Chakras

The Term "Chakras" Refers To The Idea That The Human Body Has A Number Of Energy Centers That Are Thought To Correlate To A Number Of Different Bodily Functions

Elliot Halliday

TABLE OF CONTENT

Introduction 1
Conditions Resolved Through The Use Of Reiki
.... 12
Color Therapy As A Means Of Fostering Personal Growth And Restoring Chakra Harmony 37
In Concerning The Chakras 47
What Are Mantras 56
7 Restoring Harmony To The Chakras 69
Practices For Opening And Balancing The Heart Chakra 77
How To Free Your Body Of Its 7 Latent Energy Centers 81
A Glance Into Contemporary Living 96
Your Own Internal Energy Structure 110
Acoustic Medicine 119
The Chakra Located In The Navel Region 129
The Chakra Of The Soul Star 135
Which Aspects Of Your Life Does The Heart Chakra Rule? 142

A Brief Presentation On The Chakras 145

The Seven Chakras And The Functions They Perform 151

The First Chakra 159

Having Firsthand Experience With The Strength Of Love 170

Introduction

In this book, I want to teach you the significance of opening your third eye as well as what it can achieve. Your third eye chakra is called Ajna, and it is located in the middle of your forehead. In Chapter One, I will teach you how to open your third eye and explain what exactly it is that you have there. In the second chapter, we will discuss the fundamental procedures, as well as the advantages, of reiki healing, energy healing, and chakra healing. In Chapter Three, you will learn how to obtain deeper self-knowledge and how to awaken your higher self via guided meditation. You will also learn how to do both of these things. The goal of the fourth chapter is to assist you in reaching a degree of clarity and knowledge that is superior to anything you have previously encountered. In the fifth chapter, you will learn how to get in touch with your intuition and how to keep your chakras in harmony. In Chapter Six, you will learn about some of the several methods that may be used to rid your body of bad energy. You will get a whole new lease on life as a result of the information in Chapter Seven, which will allow you to reenergize both your body and your mind. In Chapter Eight, I will demonstrate how you may utilize to repair your chakras and realign all of your chakras so that they are in harmony with one another. I will do this by using. This chapter is all about using the power of your mind to heal yourself from the inside out, lower the tension in your life, and let go of the worry you've been holding onto. You will learn how to harness the power of positive thought as well as how to cleanse your energy field in Chapter 10. You will discover guided meditations to practice throughout the whole of this book, and it is my sincere hope that you will find these sessions to be of use to you on your path. Have fun!

Your Sacred Center When it Comes to Relationships

Sometimes, maintaining healthy relationships might seem like an uphill battle. It is much too common for us to say things we later regret when we are frustrated, or to behave in unpleasant ways when we are angry. In unfortunate circumstances such as these, the Sacral shows to be of assistance. It is true that the energy of the sacral chakra is the source of our libido and intimate relationships, but it is also the source of our compassion and acceptance of others. When we allow ourselves to be guided by these aspects of the Sacral Chakra, we are able to navigate difficult confrontations with a great deal more success, and this is true regardless of whether or not these confrontations take place amongst friends, family members, spouses, or colleagues. In light of the aforementioned, give the following exercise a go the next time you find yourself in a heated discussion with someone you care about and need to keep your cool by biting your tongue:

You will need to put in some practice time before doing this exercise successfully. Don't let it get to you, however. This method is efficient and uncomplicated:

1. Devote a total of twenty minutes every week to serving as practice time.

2. Go to a place where you won't be disturbed and sit on the floor with your legs crossed.

3. Think back to a time in your life when you could have shown greater

compassion and acceptance toward other people. Imagine the specifics of the predicament in your mind. Where were you last night? Who were you with at that time? What did you have on your body? Where were you and what did you see? What have you been hearing? How did you experience it?

4. While you are doing this, put your hands on your hips and remain with them in that position for the whole twenty minute period. (The sacral region is represented by the hips, which are a component of the pelvic bone).

5. Regularly bring your attention to the fact that your hands are resting on your hips. After sufficient repetition, you'll eventually come to equate the position of your hands on your hips with the need to be more tolerant and sympathetic.

When things are very difficult, bring your hands to your hips (but be cautious). (You shouldn't make this into a hostile or defensive motion.) During times of difficulty, all that is required of us at times is a simple reminder to have compassion and acceptance for the people around us. If you have followed the steps stated above, the simple act of placing your hands for a little while on your hips should serve as a reminder of the need for you to be more welcoming and caring.

"I am in love with myself."

In utero, organ development begins with the formation of the heart. It serves as the focal point of your body. The second chakra that most people forget about is the heart chakra. It is incredibly vital, yet people often disregard its significance. When you open your Third Eye chakra, you often find that your Heart chakra remains locked. Once you have the ability to see, you could be confronted with things that your heart is unable to process. It only locks up in response to being hurt. This might cause problems in social situations or in relationships. The Heart chakra is quickly shut down by critical thinking. Grief, on the other hand, has a disproportionately negative effect on the Heart chakra. Your capacity for empathy is controlled by this chakra. Anyone who works in the medical industry or as a caregiver must understand the significance of this topic. Due to the fact that it has the greatest frequency associated with healing, this chakra is associated with the process.

It's possible that if your Heart chakra is blocked, you'll find yourself giving to others all the time. Giving up all you own without expecting anything in return. Because of this, you will feel completely fatigued. When you learn how to open the Heart chakra, you will be able to strike a healthy balance between giving and receiving, and this will leave you feeling revitalized. When you have awakened your Heart chakra, you are linked to the whole world, and as a result, you will never feel alone again.

What kinds of mental and emotional roadblocks are preventing you from opening your heart chakra? Have you been injured in the past by a member of your family or by a partner who has come and gone? Spend some time just being with yourself and your heart. If you find that seeing it as a little being helps, then do that. What is it looking for? What does it appreciate most? Is there a sense that it is appreciated or that it is undervalued? Ask it questions that are straightforward, such as "what makes you happy" or "what do you have to tell me?" Recognize the issues that it has. Give it the feedback that you believe it needs the most. Take action in order to grant its requests. After you and it have arrived at a mutually satisfactory accord, demonstrate your gratitude to it. When you have a stronger connection with your heart, you will also have a stronger connection with your soul. It absorbs every painful experience you've ever had in your life. You need to work on strengthening the connection you have with your heart.

You need to be able to communicate how you feel to others and be honest about it. Your Heart chakra needs to hear certain noises, therefore bombard it with such sounds. Binaural beats at 341.3 Hz, the bij mantra, Yam, the sound of blowing wind, and singing bowls are the sounds you hear. When it comes to opening your heart chakra, nothing beats drinking green tea and eating other foods that are green. Put on as much green as you can reasonably manage. I would go so far as to suggest that you adorn with it as much as is humanly possible to do so. This is of the utmost significance in your private space. Spend some time in the great outdoors, preferably somewhere green and breezy. Performing acts of charity without expecting anything in return is a wonderful way to connect with others and feel love without putting undue strain on oneself. When folks are just getting started, this is a simple task for them. Visualizing yourself inhaling via your chest rather than your nose or mouth might provide immediate relief for your heart chakra. Massage is a great way to unwind and may also play a significant role in assisting you in opening your heart chakra.

Conditions Resolved Through The Use Of Reiki

One of the reasons why there is a lot of attention placed on Reiki therapy in the globe today is because more success stories are being shared about the influence that it has had. As a result, a great number of individuals are open to not just giving it a go but also making it a permanent part of their lifestyle.

If you have never tried Reiki before, and if this book is your first exposure with the subject matter, you will want to know the advantages you stand to gain by adopting this strategy. Now, if you have never tried Reiki before, you will want to know the benefits you stand to gain by adopting this method. When one considers the fact that there is such a wide variety of choices accessible online, one cannot help but ask what makes Reiki so unique.

If you have experience with Reiki or if you already knew anything about this method of healing, then you are probably interested in learning more about the specific conditions and diseases that may be treated with Reiki. In this chapter, you will learn about the many ailments that may be treated with Reiki, as well as how to attain the outcomes you want by using the correct hand positions. Since we have previously discussed the topic of self-treatment, you are already aware of the steps that need to be taken in order to provide it to yourself if you want to do so.

Reiki sessions and treatment patterns may vary, and not all of them are appropriate for treating all ailments and conditions. Therefore, before beginning a therapy procedure, you will need to be aware of the exact ailment that you are currently suffering with, as well as the kind of session to do and the appropriate hand posture to use. Let's talk about it for a little while before moving on to the many sorts of ailments that may be treated with Reiki.

When treating the whole body with Reiki, there are certain postures that are supposed to alleviate certain problems. These positions may be found all over the body. During the healing process, one may remain in these postures for an extended period of time. For these kind of issues, you merely need sessions that are fast while being constant. For instance, patients with chronic ailments may be healed after attending four sessions in a row. The severity of the condition will be the deciding factor in whether or not there will be an extension.

For other people, it could take some time before they experience instant recovery, particularly in the case of cancer, when attending appointments once a week can be necessary. In order for the receiver to experience the full benefits of Reiki, they will need to practice patience and make sure there is enough connection throughout each session.

The person who is afflicted with a sickness that causes disfigurement of the body will need to bring their second and fifth chakras into harmony. If they are coping with ailments that might potentially take their lives, they will need to direct their attention on the fifth and sixth chakras.

If an individual is struggling with paralysis or another sort of handicap, then he or she should focus on bringing the first, third, and fifth chakras into a state of balance. Treatments with Reiki are beneficial for disorders that affect the mind as well as the neurological system.

The most essential thing for you to keep in mind is that receiving Reiki therapy is not a replacement for consulting a medical professional. It is not a replacement for psychotherapy sessions, nor does it serve as a substitute to natural treatment. If you discover that you are becoming more concerned about your condition and you are unable to maintain a consistent schedule for your Reiki sessions, then you need to speak with a medical professional or go to a hospital.

The truth that is made known to us can only be seen clearly by using our inner vision.

Now that you have your feet on the ground, the next step, which is much easier, is to make sure that you are defending yourself.

Be Sure to Guard Yourself (for around one to two minutes)

Take a seat in a comfortable chair and make sure both of your feet are firmly planted on the ground.

Put your hands on your lap with the palms facing up. Put a stop to your yawning.

Take three long, calm, deep breaths and see the following in your mind:

Imagine that there is a pure, warm, white light that is floating over your head and providing you with protection. As you continue to see it, it becomes clearer and more luminous in your mind.

Bring the ball down into your head slowly while spreading the light in your thoughts into every part of your head, your neck, and all the way down through your arms and shoulders.

Drive the warm, protecting light into your heart, down through your upper body, all the way through to your feet, and into your toes. Allow this protecting white light to envelop and encircle your being completely so that you are protected from taking in any other source of energy but your own.

You've put in a lot of hard work, but now you deserve a break. Take a seat, get yourself a drink of cold water, and assess how you feel after doing so. Are you seeing that there is less tension? Take some time to savor the moment and the sense of calm that has come over you. I hope that the exercises I provide you will help you find some measure of inner calm and contentment. This is a trip that cannot be rushed since it takes some time to get there. When you make an effort to slow down and concentrate on accessing your higher awareness, you will notice that a sensation of serenity is beginning to engulf you more and more.

Recognizing the reasons why doing this task is a good idea and articulating your goals for doing it are both smart places to start. What is it that you wish you could have experienced? This technique will open up your intuitive abilities to a greater degree, and it also has the ability to offer you a clearer focus. Would you want to have greater self-awareness so that you can better manage the tension and anxiety that you experience? How would you rate your levels of creativity, from low to high? Or do you often find that you are unable to think of interesting new ideas? The opening of the ajna has several advantages, one of which is the development of your psychic abilities, such as clairvoyance and clairaudience, which give you the ability to see and hear psychically, in your mind's eye.

There are a few distinct approaches that you may take in order to open your Ajna, often known as your third eye chakra. The strategy that is described here is simply the beginning of the many possible approaches that we are going to investigate together as you continue reading. It is possible that you may need to practice this meditation method for several days in a row in order to clear the energy that is preventing your pineal gland from functioning properly. You can find "instant techniques" with a little bit of study, but really what you are doing is starting an investigation into mindfulness, healing, and awakening skills that have been dormant for a long time. Time and practice are required for this. Practice self-compassion and perseverance along the journey. There is a possibility that you may only detect a very little shift; but, the more still you are, the simpler it will be to see.

Are you prepared to go? By this point, you have completed the grounding practice, which has resulted in all of the negativity that you were harboring in your body being expelled, and you have protected yourself by encasing yourself in a bright white light. As well as ensuring that you are warm and comfortable, you should also switch off your phone. Make sure there is a drink of water waiting for you at the conclusion of your session, but the most important thing is to remain calm and open to the possibilities that lie ahead.

One of the reasons why there is a lot of attention placed on Reiki therapy in the globe today is because more success stories are being shared about the influence that it has had. As a result, a great number of individuals are open to not just giving it a go but also making it a permanent part of their lifestyle.

If you have never tried Reiki before, and if this book is your first exposure with the subject matter, you will want to know the advantages you stand to gain by adopting this strategy. Now, if you have never tried Reiki before, you will want to know the benefits you stand to gain by adopting this method. When one considers the fact that there is such a wide variety of choices accessible online, one cannot help but ask what makes Reiki so unique.

If you have experience with Reiki or if you already knew anything about this method of healing, then you are probably interested in learning more about the specific conditions and diseases that may be treated with Reiki. In this chapter, you will learn about the many ailments that may be treated with Reiki, as well as how to attain the outcomes you want by using the correct hand positions. Since we have previously discussed the topic of self-treatment, you are already aware of the steps that need to be taken in order to provide it to yourself if you want to do so.

Reiki sessions and treatment patterns may vary, and not all of them are appropriate for treating all ailments and conditions. Therefore, before beginning a therapy procedure, you will need to be aware of the exact ailment that you are currently suffering with, as well as the kind of session to do and the appropriate hand posture to use. Let's talk about it for a little while before moving on to the many sorts of ailments that may be treated with Reiki.

When treating the whole body with Reiki, there are certain postures that are supposed to alleviate certain problems. These positions may be found all over the body. During the healing process, one may remain in these postures for an extended period of time. For these kind of issues, you merely need sessions that are fast while being constant. For instance, patients with chronic ailments may be healed after attending four sessions in a row. The severity of the condition will be the deciding factor in whether or not there will be an extension.

For other people, it could take some time before they experience instant recovery, particularly in the case of cancer, when attending appointments once a week can be necessary. In order for the receiver to experience the full benefits of Reiki, they will need to practice patience and make sure there is enough connection throughout each session.

The person who is afflicted with a sickness that causes disfigurement of the body will need to bring their second and fifth chakras into harmony. If they are coping with ailments that might potentially take their lives, they will need to direct their attention on the fifth and sixth chakras.

If an individual is struggling with paralysis or another sort of handicap, then he or she should focus on bringing the first, third, and fifth chakras into a state of balance. Treatments with Reiki are beneficial for disorders that affect the mind as well as the neurological system.

The most essential thing for you to keep in mind is that receiving Reiki therapy is not a replacement for consulting a medical professional. It is not a replacement for psychotherapy sessions, nor does it serve as a substitute to natural treatment. If you discover that you are becoming more concerned about your condition and you are unable to maintain a consistent schedule for your Reiki sessions, then you need to speak with a medical professional or go to a hospital.

The truth that is made known to us can only be seen clearly by using our inner vision.

Now that you have your feet on the ground, the next step, which is much easier, is to make sure that you are defending yourself.

Be Sure to Guard Yourself (for around one to two minutes)

Take a seat in a comfortable chair and make sure both of your feet are firmly planted on the ground.

Put your hands on your lap with the palms facing up. Put a stop to your yawning.

Take three long, calm, deep breaths and see the following in your mind:

Imagine that there is a pure, warm, white light that is floating over your head and providing you with protection. As you continue to see it, it becomes clearer and more luminous in your mind.

Bring the ball down into your head slowly while spreading the light in your thoughts into every part of your head, your neck, and all the way down through your arms and shoulders.

Drive the warm, protecting light into your heart, down through your upper body, all the way through to your feet, and into your toes. Allow this protecting white light to envelop and encircle your being completely so that you are protected from taking in any other source of energy but your own.

You've put in a lot of hard work, but now you deserve a break. Take a seat, get yourself a drink of cold water, and assess how you feel after doing so. Are you seeing that there is less tension? Take some time to savor the moment and the sense of calm that has come over you. I hope that the exercises I provide you will help you find some measure of inner calm and contentment. This is a trip that cannot be rushed since it takes some time to get there. When you make an effort to slow down and concentrate on accessing your higher awareness, you will notice that a sensation of serenity is beginning to engulf you more and more.

Recognizing the reasons why doing this task is a good idea and articulating your goals for doing it are both smart places to start. What is it that you wish you could have experienced? This technique will open up your intuitive abilities to a greater degree, and it also has the ability to offer you a clearer focus. Would you want to have greater self-awareness so that you can better manage the tension and anxiety that you experience? How would you rate your levels of creativity, from low to high? Or do you often find that you are unable to think of interesting new ideas? The opening of the ajna has several advantages, one of which is the development of your psychic abilities, such as clairvoyance and clairaudience, which give you the ability to see and hear psychically, in your mind's eye.

There are a few distinct approaches that you may take in order to open your Ajna, often known as your third eye chakra. The strategy that is described here is simply the beginning of the many possible approaches that we are going to investigate together as you continue reading. It is possible that you may need to practice this meditation method for several days in a row in order to clear the energy that is preventing your pineal gland from functioning properly. You can find "instant techniques" with a little bit of study, but really what you are doing is starting an investigation into mindfulness, healing, and awakening skills that have been dormant for a long time. Time and practice are required for this. Practice self-compassion and perseverance along the journey. There is a possibility that you may only detect a very little shift; but, the more still you are, the simpler it will be to see.

Are you prepared to go? By this point, you have completed the grounding practice, which has resulted in all of the negativity that you were harboring in your body being expelled, and you have protected yourself by encasing yourself in a bright white light. As well as ensuring that you are warm and comfortable, you should also switch off your phone. Make sure there is a drink of water waiting for you at the conclusion of your session, but the most important thing is to remain calm and open to the possibilities that lie ahead.

Assessing the State of the Chakras

There is, fortunately, a very simple method that can be used to evaluate chakra imbalances in addition to evaluating oneself using the aforementioned list of symptoms.

You will just need a pendulum for this.

You may 'ask' for the size, speed, and direction of each chakra by holding a pendulum above the chakra in question while dangling a crystal, stone, or other preferred dowsing item from some thin rope. You may evaluate each one using this simple way to determine if any of them are spinning too quickly or too slowly, and whether some of them are too huge or inadequately little.

Put the pendulum over each chakra, and while doing so, ask yourself questions about its health and status. At the same time, pay attention to whether or not you feel any lingering heat, cold, discomfort, or illness.

By holding the pendulum over each chakra and asking for the results, you may also use the same method to determine which stone, crystal, color, or medication is most suited for that particular chakra.

Instruments for Restoring Harmony to the Chakras

You may utilize any one of the following tools to help you become healthier, more balanced, and more confident, or you can use a mix of the techniques described below:

Therapy based on colors

The term "crystals"

Reiki is practiced via meditation and mental imagery.

Diet

Yoga

Think positively and repeat positive affirmations.

Exercice in its many forms

The practice of aromatherapy

Color Therapy As A Means Of Fostering Personal Growth And Restoring Chakra Harmony

Because the chakras have such a strong connection to color, as was discussed in a previous chapter, they gain a lot from the practice of Color Therapy, which is a method that helps develop and rebalance your seven different energy centers. In the following stages, you will be taught how to use a color bath to realign and rebalance your chakras.

RESTORING THE BALANCE OF YOUR CHAKRAS WITH THE HELP OF A COLOR BATH

Let's get started by doing a color bath for your top chakra.
Exercise for the Crown Chakra:

To start, choose a comfortable sitting position. Take a long, deep breath in and exhale through your mouth after inhaling through your nose. Repeat this process three times. Now, visualize the white light of God and the love of the Universe swirling around you in a clockwise direction, beginning at your feet and rising up towards your head. This motion should begin at the base of your feet and end at the crown of your head. Imagine that a white light is travelling around you in a circular pattern three times, each time beginning at your feet and working its way progressively upwards to your head.

Imagine a pulsating purple light moving around a little bit above your head; this is the location of your CROWN chakra. Imagine that this light is moving in a direction opposite to that of the clock. If you are getting the impression that this isn't quite correct, try visualizing the light moving in a clockwise direction instead. Do you find it simple to move this light, or does it seem to be trapped, making it harder to swirl around? If you feel as if it is "stuck," continue to see the light swirling in the direction that you have selected, whether it be clockwise or counterclockwise.

Imagine that the purple light is now circling around you in a clockwise direction or moving down towards your feet. Imagine the violet light whirling downward toward your feet and then ascending once again. If the sensation of the purple light continuing to feel heavy or trapped, this indicates that your chakra is not functioning properly. Continue to do this every day; the more you perform this exercise, the more your crown chakra will open up, rebalance, and begin to move more easily as a result of your efforts.

Exercise for the Third Eye Chakra:

Let's move on to the third eye chakra, also known as the brow chakra, which is situated in the middle of your forehead. Your ability to access your intuition is located in the third eye chakra.

Let's start by visualizing an indigo-colored light that is either traveling in a clockwise or counter-clockwise pace, depending on whatever direction seems the simplest or most natural to you at this moment. Now envision it going until it becomes simpler to move more smoothly or clearly. This should become easier as you continue. Now, visualize the indigo light circling around your complete body in either a clockwise or counterclockwise pattern (depending on which direction you like), beginning at your head and working its way down to your feet before returning to its starting point.

Exercise for the Throat Chakra:

The following practice will concentrate on the throat chakra, which controls one's capacity for rage as well as their ability to speak for themselves. Imagine a light blue light moving in a circular manner, either in a clockwise or counterclockwise direction (again, whatever direction seems most natural to you). Keeping visualizing this until it starts moving easily is the goal. When you try out these exercises for the very first time, you shouldn't have any expectations that the chakras would feel clear, easy, or smooth. Depending on how much they have been weakened, it may take more than one attempt for your chakras to start working in a fluid and easy manner again.

Now, visualize the blue light whirling in a clockwise or counterclockwise direction as it travels down your whole body to your feet and then back up again. This process should take place in reverse.

Exercise for the Heart Chakra:

The following exercise will concentrate on the heart chakra, which is located in the middle of your chest and controls not only your capacity to love other people but also your ability to love yourself. Choose either pink or green, since these are the colors associated with the heart chakra; the next activity you do to balance your chakras should use one of these hues.

Imagine that the color you chose—either pink or green—is traveling in either a clockwise or a counterclockwise direction after you have made your selection. When you are ready, begin to move it all the way around your body, all the way down to your feet, and all the way back up to the crown of your head.

Exercise for the Solar Plexus Chakra:

Your solar plexus chakra, which is situated in your diaphragm, is also very closely associated with your emotions. This chakra has a golden hue to its coloration. Again, see a yellow light spinning in a circular motion, this time in either a clockwise or counterclockwise direction, depending on your own choice. Once again, whenever you feel ready, proceed by whirling the yellow light around your body in a clockwise direction, starting at the top of your head and working your way down to your feet.

Exercise for the Sacral Chakra:

The color orange represents the sacral chakra, which is associated with sexuality. Having stated that, visualize an orange light that is traveling in either the clockwise or counterclockwise direction. Once again, when you are ready, swirl the orange light around your body, traveling in an upward direction to the top of your head, and then flowing downward to your feet.

Exercise for the Root Chakra:

In conclusion, the color red represents the root chakra, which is associated with feeling comfortable and secure in all parts of your life. This chakra is located at the base of the spine. Your pelvic region is the location of the root chakra, which stands for the roots of your family and where you came from. For the sake of this exercise, visualize a crimson light whirling about in the region of your body that contains this chakra; in this example, the area of your pelvis. After that, move this light in a spiral motion all the way down and back up your body.

A human being has to have a balance between the upward flow of energy and the downward flow of energy in order to be entire, which includes feeling like they are in excellent form both mentally and physically. The purpose of these exercises is to increase the flow of energy through the chakras, making it possible for it to flow more freely and with greater ease, which ultimately results in the chakras being more balanced and better.

If you meditate with Color Therapy and frequently practice these exercises, the healing color and light of the universe will be brought into your spiritual being. As a result, you will feel happier, healthier, more serene, and more able to easily take control over the problems that are now occurring in your life.

In Concerning The Chakras

It is the Sanskrit word for circular things, which is interesting to note from an etymological point of view. Over the course of more than five millennia, the concept of chakras has served as a cornerstone of traditional Ayurvedic treatment. Chakras are an essential component of Buddhist and Hindu belief systems. They identify the locations at which energy pathways converge to form an energetic vortex that is part of the "subtle body" of the human being but is unseen to the naked sight.

These intersection locations are also used in the practice of traditional Chinese medicine, most notably acupuncture. Some people believe that the energy of the etheric life force is represented by the chakras, and that the chakras also make up a portion of the soul. The primary purpose of these channels is to facilitate the flow of vital energy (which may also be referred to as prana or chi) from one bodily organ to another. They constitute a bridge between the spiritual and the physical, and when aligned on the spine, they perform functions that are complimentary to one another and depending on one another.

CHAKRA, IN THE MEANING OF

The Chakra is often referred to as a wheel. Similar to a wheel that revolves and may whisk objects away, or a vehicle that kicks up a cloud of dirt. Prana, which literally translates to "life energy," is what the wheel-shaped Chakra emanates. In certain traditions, the chakras are also referred to as patmas, which literally translates to "lotuses." In the same way that a lotus may expand, unfurl, and appear lovely, but it can also be closed like a bud, chakras can shut and yet have a lot of power and magnificence inside them. When we do yoga, the lotus flower opens, the chakra opens, and we become capable of bringing about many wonderful things.

There are a great number of chakras. During the most recent lecture, I discussed the nadis, which are channels that carry prana, also known as the life force. The nadi energy points are where the life force is kept, and they are connected to the chakras. Chakras are the names given to the energy centres that are located along the nadis. In reality, chakras are only a collective term for a variety of different energy centres. A chakra may be thought of as any location in space where prana congregates.

In Ayurveda, the chakras are known as the Marmas. Or each of the acupuncture sites corresponds to one of the chakras. A new chakra is formed whenever two nadis intersect with one another. The manner in which prana is dispersed among the nadis and how it travels from one nadi to another is controlled by this chakra.

There are a great number of chakras due to the fact that there are 72,000 nadis, each of which has a unique chakra. There is a possibility that the chakras are places of transition, via which prana travels from one nadi to another.

They are also capable of acting as power sources, known as pranic springs, which allow Prana to be absorbed. Additionally, there are chakras in the tongue that are responsible for the absorption of energy from both solid and liquid substances. The hand chakras have the ability to both take in and give forth energy in equal measure. Then there are the chakras, which are like accumulators in that they are places where energy is stored.

One may claim that all emotional centers are chakras, and that all mental capabilities are formed owing to the chakras. Chakras are also the organs of the astral body. When the chakras are fully activated, then there remain latent skills that may still be uncovered and developed.

As a result, chakras are responsible for a wide variety of effects, and in addition, they serve as the connectors between the astral body and the physical body. Some chakras have the ability to govern or exert influence on the body's organs. A person's cerebral capabilities as well as their emotions are controlled by other chakras. And once more, other chakras are only accumulators or compounds in the Pranamayakosha, which is the layer below the fines.

The magnetic field of the Earth provides an excellent illustration of the movement of energy. The energy flow enters the disk from the bottom, travels vertically over the disk, appears from the side, both up and down, and then returns to the bottom again. This describes the movement of energy via each chakra in the human body accurately.

The word is more commonly recognized today as "spiritual centers" or "points of junction of energy channels (n)," both of which are taken from a notion of Kundalini yoga and which are able to be located inside the human body. This theory postulates that there are seven primary chakras in addition to thousands of subsidiary chakras throughout the body.

It is a sign of power called a Chakra (wheel), and it may be seen in the middle of the Indian flag.

In ancient India, the term signified a disk made of gold, copper, or iron that represented the power of a Raja called a chakravarti. This is a person who controls the course of men's life by turning the wheel of their fate while holding their lives in his hands. However, it may also refer to a person who resembles the sun, or srya. The title of chakravarti or chakravartin was bestowed to a ruler who had accomplished significant military victories or the sacrifice of a horse.

The disc is the most important symbol associated with the divinity Vishnu.

The wheel is a symbol of both the structure of the worlds and the structure of the person in Hinduism. The centre of the wheel is the heart, the rays symbolize the individual's abilities, and the points of contact with the rim are the organs of perception and action.

After then, the phrase came to be used to refer to Buddha as well as the leaders of Buddhist nations, who are shown making the motion of turning the wheel of the law (dharma chakra-mudra).

Therefore, it should not come as much of a surprise to discover a depiction of a chakra on both the national symbol and the flag of India. In the beginning, the white ring included Gandhi's spinning wheel, which became a symbol of self-sufficiency due to its role as an iconic tool. After some time, it was replaced with the chakra of Ashoka, which is a symbol of Buddhism. This change occurred as a result of the influence of B. R. Ambedkar, an editor for the Indian Constitution who subsequently converted to Buddhism.

What Are Mantras

The word 'man', which means to think in Sanskrit, is where the English word 'mantra' originates from. A mantra may be a single word, a phrase, a poem, a prayer, a song, a charm, or an incantation. It can even be a whole prayer. Mantras are practiced with the intention of arriving at a state of righteousness. On both the material and the spiritual levels, mantras have a value that cannot be overstated. Because they are founded on energy, some sounds, when spoken in a certain manner and examined inside, may help one's woes go away and ensure one's redemption.

There are mantras in each and every faith and language. According to one of the hypotheses put out by the Eastern metaphysical tradition, the human body is made up of a mixture of five components, the first of which is sound. According to the findings of studies on the symbolism of sounds, vocal sounds have significance, regardless of whether or not we are conscious of that meaning, and there may be several levels of symbolic alliances associated with each sound. Therefore, even though we do not comprehend them, mantras do not lack meaning; there is no verbal utterance that is completely devoid of significance.

Altering one's state of awareness may be accomplished by meditating with the use of a mantra and reciting it over and over again, at first aloud and later in their minds. Mantras are sonic symbols, and their meaning and function are determined by the viewpoint and intelligence of the individual who repeatedly utters them. Many people believe that OM was the first sound that existed in the cosmos. It is not necessary for a person to comprehend the meaning of a mantra in order for it to have any effect. The power of mantras is mystical, and they have the ability to alter a person's state of awareness. Vocal sounds carry significance regardless of whether or not the person is aware of it.

Let's pretend for a moment that someone has insulted us or made fun of us. How do you think you would react? What effect does it have on us? What does it give birth to? It irritates us, it generates bad vibrations; we get seething feelings in our stomach, a certain pain physically, our muscles tighten up, and we feel rigid in the brain and throughout the rest of our body.

When words that are critical of us may cause psychological and physiological responses in us, then repeating words that have good vibrations from the universe can really be beneficial to us on all levels. Positive vibrations are sparked inside us as we recite mantras, and the energy fields that surround our etheric bodies serve to protect us.

The enigmatic sound symbols known as mantras are used to call upon the energies of the spiritual realm. They often include phrases like Om and Ah Hum (which is pronounced as hoong), neither of which have any significance when spoken literally. They are different frequencies of sound. To attempt to intellectually understand the significance of chanting mantras is like to driving while wearing a blindfold on a busy highway.

The incessant internal chattering and disorder that are hallmarks of the monkey mind are quelled by reciting mantras, which also assist provide peace to the mind. It is possible to see things and events in life with an open mind and no preconceived notions or judgments when the mind is silent and calm. The most of the time, we are not even aware that we are thinking.

The practice of mantras cultivates awareness and trains the intellect to be vigilant and to see things from a distance. This results in the least involvement possible and enables a person to detach from the drama that is generated by the mind. Chanting establishes a mental distance from habitual thought processes that are completely superfluous and progressively flushes away unwanted thought patterns, resulting in an empty, balanced, and serene state of mind.

Have you ever pondered the reason behind the sudden surge of energy you have when you see a specific person or go to a certain location? When you come into contact with good energy, this takes place. In a similar vein, there are certain individuals, some of whom you may not even know, who make you feel repulsed. This is a result of friction and an imbalance in their energy field, which causes this effect. They are unable to generate their own good energy, so they draw it from others around them and their surroundings. As a result, folks who are in close proximity to these individuals report feeling depleted.

People like this are sometimes referred to as "psychic vampires." It is possible to ward off psychic vampires by maintaining a reservoir of good energy inside oneself and being concentrated within one's own consciousness. A positive person has the ability to influence the awareness of others around them, which in turn has the effect of bettering the surroundings. Those who have engaged in the practice of self-inquiry for an extended length of time, as well as saints and realized beings, are constantly surrounded by such an aura. Additionally, children exude an atmosphere of innocence.

If you are new to the practice of mantras and meditation, it is recommended that you begin by chanting the mantra aloud.

This will prevent you from nodding off during your meditation session or letting your mind wander while you are trying to focus. Keep track of your breath and synchronize your chanting with your conscious inhalations and exhalations. While you are becoming more attuned to the methods, you may choose to repeat the mantras in your head by paying attention to your breathing.

What exactly are the Chakras?

Simply said, a chakra is the location at where the spirit and the physical body are connected to one another. The term "chakra" comes from a Sanskrit phrase that translates to "wheels of light." These "wheels of light" are the energy centers that are located throughout the human body. Each chakra has a certain function and is associated with a particular component of your body, mind, and spirit. One further way to think about chakras is as the portals through which awareness travels. Each of the chakras has a spiritual lesson that, when fully internalized, may pave the way to a more evolved state of awareness.

Because chakras are analogous to spinning wheels filled with unadulterated radiant light, both the pace at which they spin and the direction in which they spin are indicators of how well or open we are. Additionally, chakras perform the function of the body's antenna, picking up a vast range of energy information that you may or might not consciously be aware of or choose to make use of. You may be wondering why this is the case. The reason behind this is because the human body acts as an electric point through which waves and electric vibrations may travel. They react to the information that they are tuned to, which is sent to them by vibrations. The information is transmitted to them. They work on the same principle as a radio, which is that if the signal is not clear or not on the proper frequency, there will be static. Similarly, an out of tune chakra may create issues if it is used in a way that is not appropriate for it.

Transformers are another function that chakras and auras do. They connect different portions of the physical body to its non-physical counterparts and intercept energy with a vibrational frequency that is comparable to their own. If you allow any bad energy to enter the chakra, it will cause problems in your body, either psychologically, spiritually, or even physically in the form of an illness. This indicates that your chakras and auras have the potential to do severe harm to your body at times, and the only way to stop harmful energy from entering your chakras and auras is to ensure that they are in a state of harmonious equilibrium. You have to transfer the energy in your chakras in order to prevent it from having a detrimental effect on your life, which might even lead to your death.

Additionally, chakras are the entryways for the flow of mental, emotional, and spiritual energy into one's bodily manifestation. This simply means that they are the conduits via which your belief systems and attitudes flow into and shape the structure of your body and mind. Following its journey through the chakras, the energy that you generate as a result of your mental attitudes and the emotions you experience is then sent to your organs, tissues, and cells. You are now in a better position to comprehend how you influence your body, mind, and circumstances, and whether those effects are for the better or for the worse as a result of your newfound knowledge.

It is generally accepted that every person has seven basic chakras, which together comprise the human energy system. Each reflex region in your body is said to connect to a particular chakra. Let's take a look at each of these seven chakras in further detail.

But before we go into it, I want to acknowledge that the term "aura" could seem strange to you. Permit me to provide a quick explanation.

It appears as if everything around us is vibrating at an ever-changing rate. This occurs not just on the things that are visible to our naked eyes but also on those things that are invisible to them. For example, every atom and every portion included inside it, as well as our thoughts and even our own awareness, are always vibrating in some way. An aura is the electro-photonic vibration response that every item has when subjected to any external stimulation (light is one of the sources of the external excitation). This is why an aura is described as the electro-photonic vibration response.

This aura extends outward from your physical body at a distance of around three feet; however, some individuals have auras that are far larger than this; for example, survivors of rape or incest have auras that extend approximately fifty feet around them. What you understand to be your own space is the region that is inhabited by the aura. When someone is too near to you, you will often receive the impression that they are trying to invade your personal space or drain your vitality. The explanation for this is very straightforward: they are located inside your aura. Someone whose aura extends up to fifty feet will, therefore, constantly get the sensation that others are invading their space, even though those other individuals are physically quite far away.

A variety of hues may be seen emanating from living objects, including people in particular, depending on the state of their physical and mental health at any given moment. Simply put, this implies that our auras are our unique spiritual signatures, which we are unable to imitate even if we try. This, in turn, indicates that you are able to perceive someone's thoughts even before that person is able to verbalize them. In this situation, it is obvious when someone is trying to deceive you. In this context, those who have a clear, brilliant aura are those who are spiritually enlightened and have good intents, and it does not matter whether or not these people are conscious of their aura. However, regardless of how articulate, well dressed, or well looking a person may seem to be, if they have a black or gray aura, it is safe to assume that they have bad intentions.

Chakras will now be the subject of our attention.

7 Restoring Harmony To The Chakras

In the western world of the 21st century, our mindset is mostly materialistic, even in societies who practice spirituality, yoga, or the New Age. Both existence and evolution are seen to have a causal connection to the physical world.

On the other hand, the thinking frameworks of the East identify spirituality as causation. Therefore, the only way to achieve the most profound healing is via the practice of spiritual disciplines.

Tantra suggests that we may restore harmony to the Chakras by harmonizing the components that make up our individual Chakra system with the cosmic energies that govern the cosmos.

Meditation practices that assist to balance the Chakras include focusing on the color, form, sound, and energies associated with the element.

As was said before, each Chakra represents the microcosmic representation of one of the five cosmic elements (for more information on this topic, read "Powers of the Tattvas" by Woodroffe).

These components are the "stuff" that is responsible for forming the visible cosmos.

Tantric philosophy holds that all parts of the cosmos are constantly vibrating, and that these vibrations give rise to particular forms, colors, and sounds.

It is necessary to bring your Chakras into harmony with the cosmic vibrations of the global elements in order to achieve Chakra balance.

The method in which the cosmos arranges itself inside you is referred to as your chakras. They make up the framework of the "drop" that is Brahman.

Therefore, if you want to progress, you have no choice but to engage in intuitive work with the chakras and the elements.

Tantric writings have some variances, but generally speaking, the following is a list of the colors, forms, and noises associated with the Chakras:

The ChakraSeventh Grade: Color Shape SoundNothing to see, nothing to touch, nothing to hear

Sixth, neither color nor formOm or Tham?

Iridescent on the 5thNumerous formsHam

4thhues of smoky greenThe third hexagon of YamThe Second Edition of the Red Triangle RamIt'swhite.The first gold square vam was the crescent moon vam.

Your chakras are said to be in balance when the vibrations of your elements are in accord with those of the cosmos.

Tantric yoga is practiced in the manner described below. In the practice of yoga, correcting imbalances in the chakras is the yogi's life's work.

Actually, "imbalances" in your chakras indicate that you do exist. Tantrics believe that the purpose of life is to correct these imbalances as they appear along one's journey.

Meditation on the chakras is an important part of the Tantric practice of yoga, which is used to bring the chakras into equilibrium.

Mudras are a kind of symbolic hand gesture.

Gregorian chanting

Lifestyle and dietary choices

Asanas, also known as poses

Integrity (Yama and Niyama) and Selfless Service

You have to have an effect on the neuroendocrine system in order to change someone's state of mind. This may be accomplished by practices such as meditation, ideation, intention, treatment, medications, etc...

Asanas have the potential to have an effect on the neuroendocrine system as well.

When you repeat an asana, you apply prolonged and particular pressure to a gland, which in turn pumps blood and lymphatic fluid through the gland as well as the tissue that surrounds the gland. You may compare this to "exercising" your glands. Both the body and the mind feel more toned and balanced as a result of its effects.

Repeating asanas causes the central nervous system to receive gentle pulses. Additionally, it produces neuromuscular pathways that are more functioning. By clearing up space within the structure, these pathways make it possible for prana to go through the nadis with greater ease. The mind is said to be "freed up."

In addition, repeating poses helps to strengthen muscles, encourages healthy movement patterns, and reduces pain felt throughout the body.

• Focus the attention on the Chakra that you are focusing on while you are doing the asanas. This will help you get greater outcomes.

• Strive to maintain the positions.

• Perform your routine once every 24 hours for optimal results.

- Asanas are more beneficial when accompanied by a "clean" diet.

Since we are now broadly aware of what the Chakras are, how they function, and how to bring them into balance, let us investigate what each Chakra is and what it signifies on its own...

Practices For Opening And Balancing The Heart Chakra

Meditation on the Heart Chakra 1

Put yourself in a position where you can sit comfortably, either on the ground or on a chair with your feet firmly planted on the ground. Keep your posture correct by keeping your back straight without becoming tense. Put your hands on your lap with the palms facing up; this will help you be more ready to take what is being offered. You should take a few deep breaths, in through your nose and out through your mouth, and then gently shut your eyes. Examine your whole body in search of regions of stress, giving close attention to your chest region if you have any symptoms of tightness or constriction there. Continue to breathe into those regions until you can feel a release beginning to take place.

Focus your awareness on the heart chakra, which is located in the middle of your chest, when you are feeling calm and at ease. Visualize the air entering this chakra from your nose as you inhale, and the air leaving your body as you exhale moving back up your spine and out.

Imagine that your heart chakra is home to a beautiful green lotus flower with 12 petals that are all securely closed. As you breathe into your heart chakra, the lotus flower will start to light with each inhalation that you take. Its petals start to unfold with each inhalation that it takes. Keep directing your breath into your heart chakra until the lotus has completely opened up so that it can both take in and send forth love.

When your heart chakra has reached its full potential, you may start to repeat the seed sound YAM with each breath. An emerald green light starts to radiate forth from the lotus flower as you continue to chant. When you take a breath in, the prana, or universal love, is carried by the air into your heart chakra, which then causes the light to become even more intense. When you exhale, the love in your heart chakra expands and extends forth, filling first your complete body and then the space surrounding you. This happens with each breath you take. Imagine that the light is now extending even farther, through your town, across your nation, and finally engulfing the whole planet with the light of cosmic love.

Continue with this rhythm of breathing and imagery until you feel the warmth of prana's love filling and issuing from your heart chakra, where it is being accepted and given in equal measure. Imagine that the green light is gently returning to your heart chakra, where it waits, ready to be transported again on the air of your breath, when you are ready to bring your meditation to a close. Do this by visualizing the light gradually fading away. Let go of the vision, and take several nice, deep breaths while you close your eyes. Move your fingers, toes, and neck from side to side while also wiggle your fingers and toes. Once you feel prepared, you should open your eyes and go back into the room.

Perform this meditation whenever you experience a blockage in the natural flow of love in your life.

How To Free Your Body Of Its 7 Latent Energy Centers

It's possible that you're not aware of it, yet everyone of us individually have an energy field that permeates our bodies and is segmented into numerous zones. You may not know about this. The seven chakras are the actual energy centers, and they are the ones that are most well recognized. Your life will be filled with greater exhilaration, creativity, and joy if you open these seven energy focuses.

This electromagnetic energy field, which is also referred to as an emanation, is not visible to the naked eye since it is an emission. Even if it's possible that you didn't see it, you definitely would have felt it in the end. For instance, have you ever dedicated your time and effort with someone who had a pessimistic viewpoint? This person maintained control of the conversation, and the primary focus of the conversation was on the many aspects of this person's life that were problematic at the moment. Your friend will thank you at the end of the visit and tell you that they feel a great deal better after having a conversation with you, while you will walk away feeling like your energy has been spent.

Because they have strengthened their own energy field while depleting yours, they are able to feel better as a result. You will have the ability to manage the potent energy of your seven energy foci and prevent this sort of depletion if you become a Reiki Master. This ability will come about as a result of your training to become a Reiki Master.

The following is a list of the seven energy foci that run down the spine:

the first Chakra may be located just below the tailbone.

the second Chakra is located near the base of the spine, in the space between the pelvic bones.

The third Chakra is located just below the navel.

the fourth Chakra, located right next to your heart

The fifth Chakra is located at the back of the throat.

sixth Chakra: located in the middle of the cerebrum

seventh Chakra — located straight above the head, on top of the crown

These energy centers, or chakras, are interconnected and exert influence on many parts of our anatomy.

When we think about reiki, we think of spiritual energy and in-depth healing, but in reality, it is a great deal more than that. Make use of Reiki to clear out any obstructions in your chakras and sufficiently energize them. It also has a wide variety of other applications, such as assisting you in determining your true purpose or recovering from traumas sustained in the past. After you have opened all of your chakras and restored your vital energy, you will notice that life takes on a new level of significance. You develop into a person who is more vivacious, kind, and appreciative of life, and this quality is reflected in your day-to-day activities, which cause you to think about the people in your immediate environment. Learning Reiki is an investment not just in your own well-being but also in the well-being of those closest to you, including your friends and loved ones. It's possible that you don't believe you have enough energy, but the truth is that you do. It is similar to anything else, you will need to dedicate some time to learning it, but thankfully, it is quick and easy to pick up.

Unlocking Your Psychic Capabilities

Everyone has a certain amount of psychic ability. However, there are certain persons who have greater intellectual potential than others and possess more skills. Even though everyone has at least a small bit of supernatural energy, 99.9% of people do not open their power and allow it to go to waste. This is despite the fact that everyone possesses at least a little bit of supernatural energy. It's conceivable that they don't believe they have psychic ability, or that they aren't aware of how to tap into it. Both of these are possibilities. Make every effort to prevent it from coming to pass.

Open Your Mind to Psychic Capabilities

Discovering how to harness your psychic strength may improve your life by allowing you to make use of supernatural abilities such as clairvoyance, perceptiveness, astral travel, clear imagining, psychomancy, and clairsentience. You get the picture. Once you have access to your psychic powers, you will have the ability to quickly and easily learn how to utilize any one of the many skills that are available to you.

The "Vishuddha" Within the throat is located the Throat Chakra.

"A circle contained within a descending triangle" is the symbol.

Purification occurs in the Vishuddha chakra, also known as the sacral chakra.

It is connected to the ability to hear and is situated on a nerve that can be discovered in the area of the throat that is close to the pharynx. This chakra is concerned with one's capacity for learning, taking responsibility for one's own actions, having trust in oneself and one's intuition, and being creative. In the event that this particular Chakra is not healed, a wide variety of distinct physical issues may manifest in the body. This may manifest itself in a variety of ways, such as swollen glands and gums, issues with hearing, clenching and grinding of the teeth, ulcers in the mouth, and swollen glands. When this chakra is in harmony, as it should be, a person is able to have pleasant feelings and expressions, as well as strong decision-making abilities, creativity, and satisfaction in their lives. Essential oils derived from eucalyptus and sage are the ones that are thought to be most beneficial to this specific chakra.

A deficit in the throat chakra may result in anxiety, stress, and stiffness in the neck. If you want to strengthen this chakra, you need to make sure that your food is properly balanced, that you meditate on a daily basis, and that you, of course, practice yoga. Those who wish to stimulate the activity of this chakra should also keep themselves hydrated by drinking water. Shoulder openers, neck stretches, and yoga positions like the Bridge Pose and the Camel Pose are some of the other things you can do to help yourself, and they may be quite beneficial.

The Vishuddha chakra is located close to the throat, and it is responsible for regulating the mouth, gums, and teeth as well as the trachea, thyroid, vertebrae, neck, throat, esophagus, parathyroid, and hypothalamus. It has a direct impact on your feelings of safety, autonomy, self-expression, loyalty, communication, and organization, as well as the ability to plan and organize.

The effect of this chakra being out of balance may manifest as a variety of symptoms and conditions, including the common cold, fever, sore throat, swollen glands, thyroid imbalance, laryngitis, scoliosis, mouth ulcers, gum difficulties, voice troubles, teeth problems, faith, criticism, addictions, and decision-making.

Your willpower and your ability to communicate are both centered in your throat chakra. This energy area is to blame for any difficulties you have in selecting options or settling on a course of action. In addition to that, it acts as the hub of connection with a heavenly force. This spiritual power hub serves as the foundation for your religion. The throat chakra determines your capacity to speak your mind and tell the truth to others. It also controls your ability to express your ideas. If you have a healthy throat chakra, you will be able to speak your truth without being inhibited by concerns about what other people may think or say. If, on the other hand, the chakra is blocked, it will cause anxiety about how other people will respond to your viewpoints, which will ultimately lead to constraint.

Solar Plexus Chakra: The Ability to Take Action

The name "Manipura" literally translates to "city of jewels" or "lustrous gem" in Sanskrit. The graphic representation of the solar plexus chakra is a circle with 10 petals around a triangle with its tip facing downward. Both the element of fire and the transforming force of the chakra are represented by the triangle. Yellow, similar to the hue of the flame, is the color that is most often used to depict the 10 petals.

This chakra is often found at the level of the solar plexus, which is defined as the region of the body that is between the lower half of the chest and the navel. Its primary function is to assist in the transformation of materials into energy that may be used by the body as fuel, and it also assists in the regulation of metabolism.

The energy point that controls our own strength and self-confidence is located in the solar plexus chakra. The manifestation of one's will, personality, sentiments, sensitivity, and mental talents are the defining characteristics of it. From this very spot, knowledge pours out into the world. Where do you get the sense that something isn't quite right or that things aren't going to go as planned in the circumstances in which you have a premonition that things won't go well? The overwhelming majority of individuals have what is known as a "gut feeling," which comes from the word "gut."

The element of fire is most closely related with the solar plexus chakra; however, some alternative healing therapies link it to the element of air instead. It has a connection to all types of power, including the energy that comes from the sun, heat, and light. The chakra has a golden appearance to it. Because it is connected to the quality of fire, it may also be shown as a color that is somewhere between yellow and reddish orange.

In order to restore equilibrium to the Solar Plexus chakra, we have to purge ourselves of any and all disappointments that lie deep inside us. We have to let go of our remorse and come to terms with the fact that our imperfections are an integral part of the complexity that makes us entire.

The Solar Plexus Chakra and Different Approaches to Health and Healing

Yellow is the color.

Fire is the element.

Position: Beginning at the middle of the navel and continuing all the way up to the breastbone (the point where the ribs meet).

Blockages may cause a variety of emotional conditions, including anxiety, nightmares, sleeplessness, eating disorders, inclinations toward jealousy or aggression, and a lack of sensation.

Heartburn, stomach troubles, and being overweight are examples of physical ailments that may result from blockages.

Yellow citrine, tiger's eye, rainbow fluorite, chrysoberyl, cat's eye, bronzite, amber, and yellow jasper are some of the crystals that may be used for healing.

Chamomile, fennel, and juniper are some of the herbs used for medicinal purposes.

The Bach Method of Healing Impatiens, Hornbeam, and Scleranthus are some of the flowers used in flower therapy.

Anise, chamomile, lavender, lemon, and myrrh are some of the essential oils that may be used for healing.

Using sound therapy, chant the "RAM" sound, which is the "universal seed sound."

Affirmations for healing: "I am successful in achieving all of the goals that I set, and I have faith in my decisions." "My inner fortitude leads the way for me to contribute to making this world a better place."

When you wear the color yellow, you are activating the Solar Plexus Chakra. Listen to music that is romantic, talk about how you feel, and unwind in front of a fire or candles while taking slow, deep breaths into your stomach.

Position for Meditation and Yoga: the Plank

A Glance Into Contemporary Living

These days, getting things done as quickly, laboriously, and as soon as possible is the most important thing. The issue with it is that a lot of folks are clueless about how to disconnect or take things more slowly. This is going to end up having really negative consequences for us in the long run. We have never been more overweight, under more stress, or in worse health than we are right now. All of this is directly connected to the fact that we are not living healthy lifestyles and that we are unable to stay one step ahead of the curve in terms of our wellbeing. This indicates that we need to make the time to step away from the computer, as well as know when it is appropriate to do so and how to do so effectively. It should come as no surprise that many individuals do not have a healthy balance in their life given that the majority of us now spend more than 12 hours a day in front of a computer.

Numerous studies have conclusively shown that you will never be able to recuperate from the pressures of your week if you do not allow yourself some time to relax and include some sunshine into your daily routine. Do you feel that you are working all the time, even when you are supposed to be relaxing? Do you continually check your email and never take a break, despite the fact that you know this behavior is detrimental to your health? When you need to know is that you need to take some time for yourself, disconnect everything, and then charge your devices.

You need time to yourself in order to make sure that you are at your best and that you are able to recharge, much as your mobile phone needs to be connected into the wall in order to work properly. This ensures that you will have the greatest possible access to all of the materials that will assist you in achieving your goals and achieving success. You have to make sure that you schedule enough time for yourself to be able to disengage. You will be able to enjoy a more peaceful night's sleep and wake up feeling certain that your brain has been restored if you just do something as simple as turning off your mobile phone before bed. However, this indicates that you should also make preparations to terminate the connection. When you get home from work, you should not immediately start hurriedly working on your emails. This would imply that you will not be able to get access to all of the resources that you need in order to be able to refocus and recuperate from the strains that you experienced during the week.

Finding the correct equilibrium in your life will ensure that you are successful over the long run and that you will have access to all you need to be successful and happy. Without the joy that comes from inside, none of the external luxuries in the world will ever be able to make up for the void left by your lack of contentment or aid you in regaining your equilibrium and maintaining your health. For this reason, it is up to you to identify the best possible strategy to take command of both your health and your future. This responsibility falls squarely on your shoulders. Find the optimal equilibrium that provides you with everything you need to be successful in life and it will be yours for the taking.

Instructions on How to Open Your Root Chakras (Red)

You may open your chakra more effectively if you first practice grounding, which means you tie yourself to the earth. This is one of the most effective techniques to open your chakra. To do this, alter the distance between your feet so that they are shoulder-width apart and then shift your pelvis forward while bending your knees slightly. Maintaining your body's equilibrium will help you distribute your eight points equally. After you've established a connection to the earth, you should sit with your legs crossed and gently attach your index finger to your thump.

Imagine the root chakra as a closed red flower with highly potent energy shining inside it. As you focus on this chakra, the flower opens up to reveal four petals that are each full with energy. Twenty to thirty minutes should be spent contracting, holding, and releasing the perineum breath. Your root chakra ought to become more open as a result of this.

A Guide to Opening the Sacral Chakra

Beginning by sitting on your knees with an upright posture and a straightened back is the first step in opening your second chakra. Place your hands on your lap and turn them so that the undersides of your palms are facing up. Your left hand should be positioned such that it is below your right hand when you use it to touch the rear fingers of your right hand. Join the palms of both hands together at the thumps. Put your attention on the chakra and the area of the body that it symbolizes, which is located below the navel. Chant the word "VAM" in complete silence as you take slow, even breaths. You should continue doing this for at least half an hour or until you feel fully relaxed. This exercise will help you to get rid of mental clutter and will also guarantee that your sacral chakra is open.

The Solar Plexus Chakra: How to Open It

Maintain an upright position while sitting on your knees. Position your palm so that it is in front of the stomach, just below the upper belly, which is where the solar plexus chakra is situated. Put your thumps together, bring your fingers together, and then point them in the opposite direction of where you are standing. Pay attention to your chakra and the spot on your body where it is located. Chant the word "RAM" in a loud and clear voice as you keep thinking about the chakra, what it is, and what it signifies, especially how it impacts the many elements of life. Repeat this method till you are able to unwind and have a fresh feeling in your body.

How to Release Blockages and Open Your Heart Chakra

Take a seat and cross your legs in front of you. Join the tips of your index fingers in both hands to the sides of your thumbs. Put your left hand on your left knee, and your right hand should be placed just below your breastbone. Keep this posture for at least twenty minutes as you contemplate your heart chakra and its function in your body. Bring your attention to the middle of your chest and imagine what it is. While you focus your attention on your heart chakra and continue to relax, repeat the word "YAM" in your head quietly. Carry on with the exercise until you reach a point where you feel clean. After going through this procedure and opening your heart chakra, you will, after a few seconds of practice, experience a strong sensation of compassion for others.

How to Release Blockages and Open Your Throat Chakra

Once again, get down on your knees and start from there. Make a cross on the inside of each of your fingers, except the thumps. Put a connection between the tops of your thumps. At the level of the base of your neck, bring your attention to the throat chakra and what it stands for. Chant the word "HAM" in your head while keeping your focus on your throat chakra and how it relates to the rest of your life. Keep your voice low yet clear. If you do this for ten to fifteen minutes, you will experience a sense of calm and cleanliness throughout your body.

How to Awaken the Third Eye Chakra in Your Body

Put your legs across the seat. Put your hands in a position just below your breastbone. While you are touching the tops of their heads, point your middle finger away from you. Put your attention on the third eye chakra and the area of the body that it symbolizes, which is the middle of your eyes. Chant the word "AUM" or "OM" in your head quietly. As you continue to contemplate your chakra and the ways in which it influences your life, give your body permission to naturally relax. You should practice for at least twenty minutes or until you feel clean and/or stimulated to concentrate on your objectives and come up with creative ideas for how to reach them.

Concerning the area of the Sacral Chakra

The sacral chakra, also known as Svadhistana, may be found on a person's body just below the naval region. The term "Svadhistana" originates from the Sanskrit words "swa," which means "one's own," and "adhistana," which means "dwelling place within." Together, these words form the English word "Svadhistana." Deep feelings, like as desire, pleasure, and sexuality, are connected to the chakra known as Svadhistana. It is the hub of all reproductive activity. Its location around the naval region, which is a particularly sensitive area of the human body, refers to its quality as a sensory chakra. This area of the body is located in the middle of the chest. As a result of the fact that this part of the body is also the part of the body in which water is most abundant, the element that corresponds to this chakra is water.

This chakra is also known as the lover's chakra since it is mostly related with sex and the aforementioned sensations that result from sex, such as passion and pleasure. It is also known as the heart chakra because it is located at the center of the chest. Its connotations are considerably lighter than those of the Muladhara, which was covered in the chapter before this one, and it focuses more on the exploration of emotional depths like as curiosity and invigoration than on the exploration of fundamental instinctive demands. Orange is the hue that corresponds to this sensation, and the sense of taste is the one that is connected with it. The uterus, testicles, pelvis, and lower back are all under the jurisdiction of the sacral chakra.

A dark and bad feeling is controlled by each of the six petals that make up the Svadhistana image. This does not mean that meditating on the sacral chakra can remove these petals, but it may help restore balance to the energies that are contained inside the chakra. Because optimism cannot exist without the presence of negative, the feelings already do. Therefore, it is our duty as spiritual beings to take charge of our emotions, whether they be happy or bad, rather than allowing them to direct our behavior.

The Primordial Sounds Resonating Within the Sacral Chakra

The first sound of the Svadhistana is a 'vum.' One particular feeling or disposition is represented by each individual petal. The uppermost petal is referred to as 'prashraya,' and it is in charge of determining how easily you are duped. The following petal is called 'avishvasa,' and it is located below the previous one in the clockwise direction. This petal regulates the predisposition you have to distrust other people. The next petal is called 'avajna,' and it is in charge of the feeling that causes one person to look down on another person. Bewilderment is represented by the middle of the bottom petal, which is called "murchha." The next petal is called sarvanasha, and it marks the beginning of an ascent while proceeding around the flower in a clockwise orientation. This petal is the one a one should blame for their destructive tendencies. The ultimate petal is known as 'krurata,' and it is the one that is accountable for cruelty. If you want to meditate on a certain chakra, you should vocalize the corresponding root sound that corresponds to each of the chakra's seven petals. The first consonant of the word 'prashraya' is 'bham,' 'avishvasa' is the same as 'bham,' In Sanskrit, 'avajna' may be pronounced as 'mam,' 'murchha' as 'yam,' 'sarvanasha' as 'ram,' and 'krurata' as 'lam.'

It is stated that a person who meditates on these sounds has a great sense of self-esteem since they have vanquished all of their internal adversaries and won prosperity and light. When you focus your meditation on the sacral chakra, you let go of issues that have something to do with acceptance of the self, anti-social conduct, and co-dependency, which ultimately leads to a greater sense of self-awareness.

Your Own Internal Energy Structure

Now, we are aware that it is difficult to conceive of something that cannot be seen or x-rayed, much less come to a comprehension of what it is like. Let's take a look at the chakras and see how much we really understand about the extraordinary system that exists inside our bodies.

What what is a Chakra?

If you want, you may think of a chakra as an energy center that looks like a wheel and through which psychic and life force flows. Although they are analogous to acupuncture sites, chakras are not located somewhere in the body but have an effect on it. Instead, they are a component of your energy body, which is also often referred to as your spirit body or your subtle body. This is the same energy that provides life to your physical body and directs your intuitive thinking. There are many who believe that it is a component of your light body. In 1927, Charles W. Leadbeater put up a notion that has now gained widespread acceptance: that the chakras function via the electro-magnetic nature of our bodies. Because of this, chakras may be seen as electrical nodes or universal plug-in sites located throughout our bodies. (Leadbeater, 1927/2009) [Citation needed]

The primary chakras, which can be found in each part of your body in the region of your spine, work together to establish a communication and transit system for energy, not unlike to the way that the subway and railway systems in cities and nations function. The nadis, which are also known as energy channels, would serve as the lines along which prana (also known as light and energy) and information is transferred.

The chakras would serve as the stations (sites of transfer and transformation).

There is a hue and a frequency connected with each chakra, as well as certain gemstones, plants, and even tarot card meanings. Because each chakra is related to the essential systems and organs of your body, it has the ability to influence all aspects of your being, including your mind, body, and emotions. The general position of a chakra as well as the color it is should be remembered as the two most important aspects of this energy center. Although all of these concepts may seem confusing at first. Easy!

Healthy chakras not only emit light and energy, but they also spin, which is why they are often referred to as wheels. The chakras are often seen in people's minds as luminous lotus flowers or pools of light. A number of individuals hold the opinion that chakras are not just energy vortices but also gateways to higher levels of spiritual being and experience. Do not let this frighten you in any way. There won't be any discussion about disappearing into an other realm here. All that we want to do is get a deeper understanding of chakras, including how they function, the impact they have on our well-being, and the steps we need to take to maintain healthy chakras in order to have a healthy mind, body, and spirit.

According to many spiritual traditions, our bodies are home to 88,000 chakras. To our good fortune, contemporary spiritual practices and energy workers focus their attention on the seven primary chakra points. These hubs are arranged in a manner that is parallel to your spinal cord, and they are positioned at nerve nexus locations. We will start our tour of the chakras with the Root chakra and make our way all the way up to the Crown chakra. This will allow us to go from the chakras linked with the physical world and survival to the chakras related with the intellect and the spiritual world.

The first, or root, chakra

Given that it is the origin point of the complete chakra system, we will begin with the first chakra center. This is as good a spot as any other to begin. If you haven't brought this specific chakra center into balance, there's a good probability that the rest of your chakra centers are out of whack as well. The seventh and lowest chakra center is called the Root chakra, which is fitting given that its primary function is to provide a sense of security and stability. This implies that you will become more aware of the world around you as a result of being connected to the Earth itself. Because you CANNOT correct the other chakras until you have first brought this one into balance, balancing it first is of the highest significance and should be done more than once. The location of the Root Chakra, which in Sanskrit is referred to as the Muladhara, lies at the very bottom of your spine, at the area in between your pelvis and your tailbone. The color red is associated with this chakra.

Your innate thoughts and actions are controlled by the Muladhara, which is located in the center of your brain. This is the source of the energy that drives the "fight or flight" impulse. The second facet of your existence that it controls is how your will is manifested in the world. The effort you put into obtaining that promotion, new home or vehicle, or even a new girlfriend is propelled by the energy that is present in this place. It is important to keep in mind that this is not the same thing as the strength of your will; rather, it is the expression or result of that force. Therefore, it would be to your advantage to concentrate on this chakra center if you are aware that you will soon be confronted with a challenging objective.

Therefore, in order to know how to repair it, you first need to know that it is broken, right? Now that we've got that out of the way, let's talk about a few things that can point to an imbalance in your Root chakra. Anxiety problems, being extremely scared, and having nightmares on a regular basis should be the first things to be looked for in a person who exhibits these symptoms. There is a possibility that you may suffer none, some, or all of these symptoms, with the number of symptoms suggesting the likely severity of the internal imbalance. Problems with your colon, bladder, waste disposal, lower back, legs, or feet are some of the physical manifestations that might result when your root chakra is out of balance. Again, you may not feel all of them at the same time, but the fact that you can claim to have experienced at least three or more of them should serve as something of a warning to immediately begin balancing your Muladhara.

We are going to mention just a few of the many methods that you may enhance the health of your chakras, but this should be plenty to get you started. Spend some time investigating as many different strategies as you can while you're trying to get your chakras back into alignment. If you do this, you will increase the likelihood of discovering the strategies that are most suited to your personal abilities. Meditation is an effective method that may be used to heal the Muladhara chakra. Your meditation practice has the potential to act as a tool for anchoring you by bringing about a condition in which you are more aware of both your internal and external environments. Because the Muladhara chakra's sensory organ is the nose, bringing your attention to the tip of your nose as you meditate is an effective way to speed up the healing process for the Root chakra.

Acoustic Medicine

Mudras are ceremonial or symbolic hand gestures that are used in Buddhism and Hinduism. Chakra meditation with sounds makes use of mudras. While certain mudras are performed with the complete body, the vast majority of them are done just with the hands and fingers. It is possible for the mudras to channel more energy into the chakras.

When you recite the Sanskrit words, a resonation is produced inside your body, and this resonance may be felt in the chakra that the words are intended for.

Perform meditations lasting anywhere from seven to ten breaths while reciting the Sanskrit word corresponding to each chakra as many times as possible. You need know the following in order to correctly pronounce Sanskrit words: the letter 'A' should be spoken as in the English word 'ah,' and the letter 'M' should be pronounced as if it were the letter 'ng' in the English word 'king.'

The process of doing a sound therapy session for the purpose of enhancing chakras is outlined in the following steps.

1. To begin, you should focus on activating and balancing your root chakra so that you may build a solid foundation before moving on to balancing the other chakras. Bring your middle finger and index finger together, then use your other digit, the thumb, to touch both of your fingers together. Chant the sound LAM again and over.

2. Proceed to align your sacral chakra by first placing your hands on your laps with your palms facing up and on top of each other. 3. Next, bring your feet together and place your hands on top of each other. The palm of the left hand

should rest on the back of the right hand's fingers, and the left hand should be positioned below the right hand. Put a little touch of contact between the thumb tips. As you recite the sound VAM, bring your attention to the sacral chakra.

4. After that, you should adjust the alignment of your solar plexus chakra by positioning your hands in front of your stomach, just a little bit lower than your solar plexus. Create a tent shape with the fingers of both hands, then cross your thumbs so that the left thumb is on top of the right thumb, and finally, while maintaining that posture, chant the sound RAM.

5. To open your heart chakra, sit in a cross-legged position and bring the tips of your thumbs to the tips of the index fingers on both hands. Do this for a few

minutes. Place your right hand in front of the bottom portion of the breast bone, just slightly above the solar plexus, and breathe deeply. Focus your attention on the heart chakra, which is located at the level of the heart on the spine. YAM is the sound you should chant.

6. To begin re-establishing harmony in your throat chakra, begin by interlacing your fingers and placing your palms together. Take out your thumbs, bring them together at the tops so they just barely touch, and then bring them little closer together. Chant the word HAM while bringing your attention to the area of your neck that houses your throat chakra.

7. After some time has passed, open your third eye chakra and bring it into a state of balance by placing both of your hands in front of the bottom portion of

your breast. Straighten out the middle fingers and bring the tips of those fingers together so that they are touching as they point forward. The remaining fingers should be bowed such that the top sections of the two phalanges come into contact with one another. Position your thumbs so that they point in your direction. Bring the knuckles of both thumbs together. Concentrate your attention on your third eye chakra, which is situated just above the space in between your eyebrows. The sound AUM or OM should be chanted.

8. To finish, bring your head chakra into alignment. To begin, position your hands so that they are in front of your tummy. Allow the tips of the small fingers to contact one another as they point upward. After that, proceed to cross the rest of your fingers and tuck

your left thumb beneath your right thumb. Chant the sound NG while focusing all of your attention on the crown chakra located at the top of your head.

The following are the most efficient strategies to rid yourself of sins and bad energy:

First method: water has mystical properties.

You may ask why Christians and Muslims utilize water as a means of purification, and the answer is that there is a definitive rationale for this practice. What time did they finish? To become a Christian, the first step is baptism, which involves being submerged in water and having all of your sins washed away in the process. However, why water? And can you explain the scientific reasoning behind that? The process of cleaning and purifying the energy points in your body raises the question of why these areas even need cleansing in the first place. People get depressed or feel anxious or get to experience any kind of illness because the bad energy and blockages that have blocked you energy points completely cause you to become or feel ill. Well, in case you didn't know this, every sin and wrong thing you do creates a bad energy and blockages in your body above the energy points. Well, in case you didn't know this, I will tell you now. Therefore, water may cleanse, but it cannot purify you until you first complete an essential procedure, which is as follows:

Getting into the water with the genuine and sincere aim to cleanse one's spirit is necessary.

Nothing will take place if there is no aim behind it. People have a habit of taking showers every day without the proper purpose, which is why they end up not receiving the results they desire. On the other hand, someone who wants to be baptized will have his intention in the correct place and will be well prepared to receive purification; as a result, when he gets himself dipped into the water, he will really be cleaned and cleansed.

Before beginning the act of prayer, Muslims are required to perform a ritual known as "Wudu," which entails washing their hands, faces, mouths, ears, heads, and feet. This is done in order to cleanse and purify their energy points before to praying. Have you noticed that they concentrate on cleaning the main points, beginning with the hands, which are connected and linked to all body parts, and ending it by washing the feet, which is where the negative energy leaves the body. In between, they wipe their heads, which is the important point where you get charged directly from the divine, god of the universe. Have you noticed this?

The following verse from the Quran emphasizes the need of water in regaining one's vitality:

[21:30] of the Surah Al-Anbya: (Have those who disbelieved not pondered that the heavens and the earth were a united entity, and that We separated them, and that We produced every living creature from water? Then they won't believe, will they?

This verse is an obvious indication that water awakens and brings life into everything from your soul to your energy points to your physical body. When speaking about your physical body, this verse explains pretty well the reason behind the importance of water for all body parts, from hair growth to metabolism boost and many other aspects that you can start searching for.

Concentrate on consuming a large quantity of water, and in addition to that, wash and purify with the purpose of being cleaned and purified throughout the body and energy points. If you wash your body parts only once, it will help, but you need to do it every day because, let's face it, we are humans, and we sin every day and do things that are wrong here and there, regardless of whether we planned to do them or not.

The Chakra Located In The Navel Region

Yellow is the color associated with the navel chakra, which is said to be related to one's sense of self-assurance. You may discover enormous confidence and improve your ability to cope with other people by working with this chakra. The energy that is necessary to succeed at the highest levels of a business environment may be obtained via the navel chakra. At the same time, it is of great assistance to those who operate best in collaboration with others. Your affable personality and self-assured viewpoints will help you stand out from the crowd more than ever before.

When you open the navel chakra, you get greater control over your emotions and you activate the dignity that is already inside you. As a result of your mind's capacity to link your present issue with previously stored knowledge in your memory, it may also help you make excellent decisions fast and improve your ability to appraise diverse circumstances. This is because of how your mind works. You will be able to study and analyze a wide variety of facts in a way that is much more convenient for you than it was before you gained this new level of self-assurance.

If the yellow chakra is not functioning properly, the exact reverse may take place. When it comes to testing your abilities, you won't be able to put your faith in your gut instincts, and you'll feel perpetually uneasy about the situation. Simple issues will present themselves to you as challenging inquiries, and you will have the impression that you are unable to filter through any confusing information that you get. You will be coerced into acting in a passive manner, rendering you unable to make judgments in a timely manner.

This might lead to a lack of self-confidence as well as an inability to make a significant contribution to the society or organization that you are a part of as a consequence. Your professional life will become filled with failures, and you will suffer a significant reduction in your level of self-esteem as a result.

In a similar line, having a navel chakra that is overactive may cause you to behave in an overly aggressive and competitive manner. You will become aware of a "rush of blood" in all of your activities, which will pull you away from a state of serenity and tranquillity. Because you will continually be in a "high" state, your ability to make decisions will also be negatively impacted.

It will become extremely difficult for you to remain cool and evaluate any complicated scenario for what it really is, and as a result, you will be driven to make decisions that are inappropriate since you will be unable to evaluate the facts appropriately.

You may open your navel chakra and get all of the advantages that come with doing so by using a few simple procedures. Place your hands on your knees and sit in this position with your back straight yet relaxed. You should relax your hands and just let them dangle at your sides like that. Now, gently lift your hands over your head and place them in front of you, just below your navel, with the fingers of each hand pointing away from you. It is essential that you place your hand in this manner.

Hold your hands so that your fingers are touching each other and your thumbs are crossed. Begin to focus your attention on the navel chakra as well as the area of your spine located right above your navel. Chant "RAM" to make yourself feel more relaxed, and as you're doing so, think about the benefits of this chakra and how it may help you lead a more fulfilling life. Maintain this stance and force yourself to think of nothing but this until you have cleared your mind of everything else. Maintain this posture until you get that "clean" sensation in your body.

It is recommended that you conduct exercises for your navel chakra on a regular basis, especially if you are a working person and especially if your day-to-day existence requires you to make important choices. Something like this is conceivable for higher-level executives, whose judgments in day-to-day operations of a company may either result in significant profits for their stakeholders or in catastrophic losses for those stakeholders.

The Chakra Of The Soul Star

The Fundamentals of the Soul Star Chakra

In the same vein as the Earth Star chakra, the Soul Star chakra is one of the energy centers that the vast majority of people know very little about. Both the Earth Star and the Soul Star chakras are termed "subpersonal" chakras since they are located outside of our physical bodies. The Soul Star chakra is quite similar to the Earth Star chakra.

Our eighth chakra is located between six and twelve inches above the crown of the head. It is also known as the Seat of the Soul and is also referred to as the Soul Star chakra. It is regarded as the portal via which we may access the upper worlds and the universe. You might think of this chakra as our link to our highest self, and it functions as a conduit between embodied experience and spiritual awareness. It is known as Vyapini in Sanskrit, which literally translates to "universal heart," and it is connected to the color magenta or dazzling white.

A Soul Star Chakra That Is in Good Health

When we have a Soul Star chakra that is in a state of balance, we are able to transcend the dualistic character of existence and become one with "all that is." Because we now have a better understanding of our soul purpose, we are able to lead lives that are more congruent with who we are at our core. Beliefs that constrained us in the past are no longer an issue, and we are free to go ahead with purpose.

Disharmonies in the Soul Star Chakra

If we have a blockage in the Soul Star chakra, we may have feelings of emptiness or a sensation that something is missing from our lives. It's possible that we become trapped and can't figure out what our mission in life is. An excessive amount of energy in the eighth chakra may manifest in the same ways as an overactive Crown chakra might, including a lack of direction, detachment from the physical world and the earth, and an obsessive desire to be in a "enlightened" condition. On a more tangible level, we can have regular headaches and feelings of lightheadedness.

Where do the chakras come from?

Homo sapiens are without a doubt the most incredible beings that have ever existed. A human being's energy field is the conduit via which their life force flows. The energy force is located in this core, which is known as the chakra. The term "turning" or "wheel" in its literal sense is whence we get the word "chakra," which was borrowed from a Sanskrit word. Because they are located inside the body, some refer to them as the "wheels of life." These vortices of energy are known as chakras, and they are located at certain points throughout the human body. They are the channels via which the energy enters and exits your body, and they are represented by your auras. You are aware that detritus, leaves, litter, dirt, and waste constantly obstruct the streams and lakes, right? It is the same with the chakras since they are capable of being blocked by a variety of various sorts of energy. Because of this, it is really necessary for you to continue working on the chakras and to strive toward maintaining them clean. You will not be able to attain the utmost degree of fitness in terms of your physical appearance, spirituality, or mind until you do this, since it is the only way to do so.

The author Rosalyn Bruyere explains the connection between the auras and the chakras in her book Wheels of Light: Chakras, Auras, and the Healing Energy of the Body. Bruyere also discusses the healing energy of the body. She had said that a person should consider his or her trip to be something conventional rather than innovative. These chakras, which are filled with an incredible amount of electromagnetic energy, have been around for as long as Mother Earth has! These chakras were once a key component of long-forgotten mysteries, but those secrets have been lost to time. Another thing you will need to keep in mind is that you will find your way back to a mystery that is at least as old as the existence of life on this planet by working with these chakras. God is the subject of this age-old mystery.

As soon as you begin to focus on developing your chakras, you will realize that you are thrust into an extraordinary adventure. You will be able to focus the energy of light that is already inside you, and you will also be able to let go of any responsibilities or burdens that you may be carrying through life. When you maintain the equilibrium of your chakras, you will not only be able to keep yourself healthy but also joyful. You are going to need to work on your meditation, and you are also going to need to practice the methods that are presented in this book. You will also be able to restore balance to the energy centers that are located throughout your body. You will discover that you are capable of healing yourself on all levels, including the physical, the mental, and the spiritual. You will also have a greater capacity to comprehend oneself, and in the course of doing so, you will locate and awaken your spiritual self.

You will discover that each chakra is always connected with a color that is exclusive to it. These consistently correlate to the colors of the rainbow, with red appearing at the bottom and violet appearing at the very top. Because you are about to go through an energy vortex, you could notice that your experiences have several tiers to them.

When you are working on your chakras, you will discover that there are seven different styles of meditation that you might practice. These stretches aren't only for the chakras; everybody may benefit from them. Your body has a number of energy centers known as chakras, and you may repair and restore balance to these areas via a variety of activities. It is common practice to correlate these chakras with a person's physical, emotional, and mental well-being. However, there are a variety of schools of thought on the chakras and how they relate to certain individuals.

Which Aspects Of Your Life Does The Heart Chakra Rule?

Relationships are governed by the energy that comes from this chakra, and it is this energy that allows you to love other people. It enlightens you to the fact that self-acceptance is crucial and necessary in order to accept others, and it makes you more aware of its importance.

Your capacity for compassion, empathy, and genuine concern for the well-being of others, in addition to your own, are all within the purview of the heart chakra. Despite the fact that practitioners use this chakra rather regularly, it is also extremely commonly misinterpreted by outsiders.

The energy that emanates from this chakra may assist in the construction of bridges between two individuals, so enabling them to achieve a deeper degree of mutual understanding. To summarize, it creates the conditions in which you are able to love other people.

The Heart Chakra is also responsible for your capacity to feel compassion for others. Being compassionate toward others paves the way for one to become more accepting of oneself and others.

If you lacked compassion, it would be very difficult for you to make it in this world full of other people. Compassion enables you to abstain from casting judgment on other people even when you disagree with what they are saying or doing, which is one of the many benefits of cultivating compassion.

A Brief Presentation On The Chakras

The Chakra System Let's Begin at the Beginning: What Exactly Are the Chakras?

Our chakras function similarly to spiritual nerve-clusters and are often referred to as the organs of the soul. They assist our mind in regulating the flow of energy throughout the body. In spite of the fact that knowledge of the chakras can be found repeated across the ancient globe (from India to Japan), the name "chakra" comes from the Sanskrit language and literally translates to "wheel." This is due to the fact that when seen from an energetic perspective, each of them seems to be a blazing wheel of color and light. It may be determined how active they are as well as what effect they are having throughout your body by looking at the pace, direction, and intensity with which they spin. This practice, which is largely founded on the ancient spiritual teachings of the Mediterranean, India, China, and Japan, is referred to as energy medicine or energetic treatment by modern practitioners.

We are not distinct from spirit; rather, we are an integral part of it.

- Plotinus, a Greek Sage and Mystic from antiquity

The ancient doctors and healers of our society were aware of something that they called the Subtle Body. This concept refers to the energy that circulates inside and around our bodies, which causes specific places to be drawn to them and aids in the healthy operation of our organs. The paths that this energy travels through are referred to in Chinese medicine as meridians, and the alternative treatments of acupuncture and Chinese herbal therapy operate by manipulating these various meridians in order to cause some of them to open up while simultaneously causing others to shut.

These meridians are responsible for transporting energy from one region of the body to another by way of hundreds of chakra points, which are often located close to or directly above glands, nerve clusters, and important organs. However, there are seven locations across the body where all of these Meridians come together to create the Major Chakras. These are the Chakras that manage not only certain parts of the body but the whole body as a whole.

These primary energy centers actively and passively draw energy from the surrounding environment in order to power our bodies. They get their vitality from the sun, the fresh air, and the natural cycles of night and day. In addition, they get their energy from the food that we consume and the habits and routines that we follow. If we are healthy, then the energy in our meridians moves freely and the "wheels" of our chakras are spinning, which maintains a consistent level of wellness throughout our whole body. Similar to the pulmonary blood systems, their normal condition is to be one in which they are turning, churning, recycling, and replenishing the energy.

For a variety of reasons, which we shall elaborate on in the next section, people have long held the belief that certain Chakras are responsible for regulating different emotional patterns and states of being as well. In practice, you may create a beneficial and immediate impact on your self-confidence, physical health, and professional accomplishments by balancing your chakras.

Chakras are the points that the Hindu religion regards as the regions that need to enable energy to flow through the body. Similar to how acupuncture depends on particular spots in the body to aid the flow of yin and yang, the Hindu religion sees these points as the areas that need to allow energy to flow through the body. These are positioned in the manner shown in the following figure, and each one is associated with a different body function.

Let's go over what they are, so that you can have a better grasp on what they include and how they work. The Crown Chakra is, of course, the finest location to begin, since it is situated in about the same area that one may picture a halo to be positioned. It's possible that you're even thinking about an aura at this point.

The Seven Chakras And The Functions They Perform

Westerners are primarily acquainted with the chakra system that consists of seven chakras. Having said that, there is just one chakra system, which is something that even a newbie should be aware of. While some systems identify hundreds of main chakras, some only identify five of them. Each of these approaches to philosophy and spirituality has its own unique insights to offer, yet none of them are inherently flawed.

Both the alternative system and the system that lists many extra centers contain the five chakras in both the seven chakra system and the system that lists many other centers. This is comparable to stating that the body consists of five primary systems: the brain, the throat, the lungs, the stomach, and the liver.

All of the items on the list play a significant role in the way the body functions. We may make that number seven by including the eyes and the reproductive system. When we examine the body on a cellular level, however, we find that this is still just a tiny fraction of the intricate biological machine that humans are. This intricate machine consists of several nerve centers, bones, joints, blood arteries, intestines, and a great deal of other components.

However, if you are instructing a youngster or a medical student who is just starting out about the many parts of the body, you do not begin by bombarding the student with list after list of the Latin names for the various bodily parts. On the other hand, you start with the main systems and how they function. Similarly, this is also the case while learning about the chakras. When we concentrate on the seven-chakra system, we are able to get a clear understanding of the locations of the chakras as well as the primary roles that each of them plays. As soon as they are mastered, it is simple to go to systems that are more complicated or provide alternatives.

Imagine that you are sat on a resilient surface, like a yoga mat or a gym mat, in either the lotus position or cross-legged posture. This will help you comprehend how these seven chakras connect to the different parts of the body.

Your Root Chakra is located at the base of your spine, at the portion of your body that is in touch with whatever you are sitting or standing on. It symbolizes the pillars upon which your existence is built, including the provision of food, housing, and money — in other words, all that is necessary for maintaining one's physical health. If you are in a standing stance, it establishes a connection with the nerves, bone, and tissue that enable you to walk erect, or, to put it another way, that "roots" you to the soil.

The next chakra is the sacral one. Although it is situated in the middle of the abdomen, it has some similarities to the reproductive organs and functions in a similar way. Relationships, emotional steadiness, a feeling of completion, and levels of joy and happiness are all controlled by it. When you think of the function of the Sacral Chakra, the phrase "gut feeling" often comes to mind. It refers to our most fundamental, id-driven, intuitive responses to the environment that we find ourselves in.

The Solar Plexus Chakra is in charge of directing both of these subordinate spheres. Our capacity to lead and arrange our life, as well as our capacity to think things through, is governed by this skill. It is the center of our sentiments of self-esteem and self-worth, as well as our overall perspective of the world.

The next chakra is the heart chakra, which, like the three chakras that came before it, is responsible for managing and directing energy. Here is the seat of our capacity to love, to establish connections that endure, to get passionate about problems, and unfortunately, the seat of our rage, hatred, and resentment, which are there right along with the wonderful emotions that are present.

It should come as no surprise that the Throat Chakra is concerned with communication, self-expression, and the expressing of sentiments to the outside world. Its activities are not quite as complex as those of the heart, but they are very necessary – very much like the nerves and blood arteries that are positioned in the neck and that bring messages and blood to the brain.

The pituitary gland is associated with the Third Eye Chakra, often known as the brow Chakra. The third eye chakra is responsible for governing comparable spiritual reactions, much to how the pituitary gland is responsible for the secretion of hormones that regulate many of our body's activities. It is our capacity to understand how the many components of a system fit together. Some people think that it enables us to see things like auras, ghosts, and psychic imprints that have been implanted in objects. Others think that it only gives us the ability to view these things. Between the lower functions and the higher functions, it works as a gatekeeper.

In some ways, the Crown Chakra is analogous to the pineal gland, which is another essential component of our endocrine system. On the other hand, the Crown Chakra is analogous to the impact of Higher Beings. Consider your atheism to be the facet of your worldview that most strongly supports the idea that human flourishing is the most important thing in the universe.

In our etheric envelope, the seven chakras are the primary or major energy centers or systems. You may also think of them as a mnemonic device for the physical systems that make up our bodies. Either style of thinking will operate well; the important thing is to choose a strategy for consideration, one that you will be able to utilize and live with. The Eastern ideologies as well as the Hindu practices include the chakras into their systems.

However, similar to the practice of yoga, you are not need to subscribe to those points of view in order to make use of the chakras as a tool to enhance your mental and emotional steadiness in addition to your bodily well-being. The system is not constrained by any one religion and collaborates directly with us in our natural state.

You may discover that it is helpful to get a coloring book that has images of each of the main chakras as you go through the many chakras, and you can do this by purchasing such a book.

The First Chakra

The Root Chakra, also known as the Base Chakra, is the first of the seven chakras and may be found near the base of the spine. It is physically located somewhere along the portion of the tailbone that is placed between the anal exit and the genital organ. This area is known as the perineum. The Root Chakra, which is also referred to as the Muladhara Chakra, is the center of support. It is a symbol of the basis upon which a person is built.

There is a connection between the Root chakra and three different nadis. Ida, Pingala, and Sushumna are the names of these three. These nadis have their beginning in the Root Chakra, and they are responsible for transporting both the vital energy (known as prana shako) and the mental power (known as manas shako) throughout the body.

Everything that has to do with sustaining one's life is the domain of the Root Chakra. Because it provides you with the sensation of being rooted in the Earth, it has a connection to the planet. It controls sexuality, stability, sensuality, and a feeling of safety in addition to governing sexuality.

Emotional concerns relating to one's ability to endure are those that are associated with this chakra. It is concerned with issues relating to work security, financial stability, and the capacity to make a livelihood for oneself. You are experiencing issues with your Root chakra if you find that you are always questioning whether you have enough money to purchase food, pay the rent, or spend it on anything you need. When you are concerned about whether or not you have the support of family and friends, the same thing may be stated. However, you need to have an understanding of the true source of the assistance. It is derived from the planet itself. In order to become grounded and to free yourself from anxiety over your safety and ability to survive, you must maintain a clean first chakra.

Fear, bewilderment, and worry are the results of an unbalanced or blocked Root chakra, which you might manifest if you do not clear it. It is also possible for it to manifest as feelings of abandonment, melancholy, or hopelessness. Another symptom of a blocked Muladhara is fear, namely fear of one's own safety or the sensation that one is in danger. On a physical level, it could manifest as a lack of energy, discomfort, impotence, and medical concerns relating to the skin.

dread prevents Muladhara from functioning properly; more particularly, the dread of not being safe or of lacking the resources necessary to continue living. You are anxious about your own ability to live. To activate this chakra, you must first identify the thing that scares you the most. You need to find out your worries in the same way that Guru Pathik instructed Aang to do. You have to have a better understanding of your worries. You have no choice but to let go of those worries and watch them go down the brook. Put aside your worries and have faith that you can triumph over any obstacle standing in the way of your safety and wellbeing.

You need to direct your attention to the spot where your Base Chakra is situated in order to assist cleanse it. Take a seat and try some meditation. You should close your eyes and picture a ball of energy radiating from your perineum or tailbone. Imagine for a moment suppose the ball was colored crimson. It is the hue of the Shakti, and it represents coming into one's own. The color red best represents the earth. It is a symbol of the abundance that exists on our planet.

You may chant the sound "LAM" and repeat an affirmation while you are meditating on the Root chakra and envisioning that ball of fire that is red in color. Repeat the following phrase as often as possible: "I am rooted. I have backing in this."

In addition to the practice of meditation, you might also engage in physical activities such as jogging, running, or yoga. Because they make you more conscious of your body, physical activities of any kind help you become more in tune with it, which in turn helps cleanse the Root chakra.

People often fail to appreciate the significance of the ground they walk on. They fail to understand its significance the vast majority of the time. Nevertheless, after the Earth is gone, everyone will just be floating about in the void. To clear your Root Chakra, you must first establish a connection with the earth. Stomping your feet may work wonders for unblocking your chakra, and it's a simple motion that everyone can perform. In addition to that, you may try this easy exercise:

Maintain a calm and upright stance with your feet at about shoulder-width apart. Before you move your pelvis forward, be sure that your knees are slightly bent. This might be challenging, so make sure you don't lose your equilibrium. Make sure that the soles of both feet are bearing an equal amount of your weight. Then move your weight to the front of your body. Maintain this stance for a few minutes as you gain a sense of the earth under your feet.

The Chakra referred to as the Throat (Vishuddha).

The fifth chakra may be found at the junction of the collarbone and the base of the neck. It is also known as the solar plexus chakra. It is blue in color and has to do with expressing oneself honestly, accepting responsibility for one's own requirements, and establishing one's own personal power. It embodies our means of communication, the synthesis of sounds, our capacity for self-expression, and our aspiration to both say and hear the truth. This chakra is represented as a circle contained inside a descending triangle, and the sapphire serves as its gemstone. Saturn is its planetary home, and hearing is the sense that is most closely linked with it. The solar plexus chakra functions as the spiral pair of the throat chakra.

If you have an open throat chakra, you will have little trouble expressing yourself, and this self-expression may often take the form of creative endeavors. those who have a lot of surplus energy in their throat chakra have a tendency to be more stubborn, judgemental, and authoritarian. On the other side, those who have a lack of openness in their throat chakra have a hard time expressing themselves clearly, do not talk much, and lack faith. They also have a tendency to be shy, and presumably have an introverted personality, and they have difficulty expressing their opinions for fear of being judged. When your throat chakra is in harmony, you will have feelings of creative and even musical inspiration, and you will also have excellent public speaking skills.

Having a blocked throat chakra has been linked to hyperthyroidism, back discomfort, inflammations, sore throats, ear infections, skin irritations, and other similar conditions. The thyroid gland, the teeth, the ears, and the neck are all associated with the throat chakra. The throat chakra also corresponds to the ears. In general, the throat chakra is at the core of our capacity to speak and express ourselves, not to mention the fact that it is the location where the inner voice of one's truth is spoken. It is sometimes referred to as the chakra of diplomatic relations.

Healing of the Throat Chakra

If you wish to be able to speak and express yourself better, you should look into the several ways that your throat chakra may be healed, which are explained in the following paragraphs.

Remedy via sound

This is the important key to unleashing the energy that is stored in your throat chakra. You should play sound to yourself and let it out. Practice mantras on a regular basis, sing or listen to your favorite tunes, or even chant mantras. Because reflex points on the roof of the mouth convey impulses to the brain, which in turn stimulate certain places in the body, a mantra is a particular sound that, when repeated, vibrates through the nerve system to have a direct influence on the specific chakra.

Increase the amount of natural fluids you consume.

The greatest way to heal your throat chakra and bring it back into balance is to drink fluids that have nutritional content. Take in some fresh juices and herbal teas every now and then. Your throat chakra may also be healed by eating certain fruits, notably figs, specifically.

Having Firsthand Experience With The Strength Of Love

The Anahat Chakra, also known as the Heart Chakra, is responsible for infusing us with love and assisting us in overcoming our feeling of "Me, My, and Mine." When we are able to open our heart chakra, we are able to have more meaningful connections with the people in our lives. We are allowed to communicate our concerns and feelings to one another. When other people really understand and care about us, it makes us joyful. We are now more open to the perspectives of other people and more understanding of the limits they have.

Our feeling of freedom is diminished when we try to meet the standards set by the people we care about. We all place a high value on our independence and strive to further our knowledge by making our own blunders as we pursue this goal. On the other hand, even when we make quick advances toward development on the route we've chosen, we unconsciously put our expectations on the people we care about the most. There is not the slightest shadow of a doubt in anyone's mind that we love our friends and family very much. But we just can't seem to 'Let Go' of this. Love is synonymous with liberty. Love requires making sacrifices. To love someone is to accept them just the way they are. Love is a state of inner calm, contentment, and harmony. And in order to achieve this condition of emotional equilibrium, we need to learn to 'forgive' and 'let go' of not just other people, but also our own pasts. This will need us to open the heart chakra.

Every time we are presented with a new obstacle—which is usually on a daily basis—we have the goal of achieving this sort of equilibrium. This internal conflict is what forces us to face and triumph over the unfavorable aspects of our personalities. We have come to the conclusion that we are the cause of our own suffering because we are unwilling to acknowledge the truth and would rather cling to the obsolete ideas and beliefs that we have. We must first make the effort to alter ourselves before we can even consider attempting to alter another human being.

Beneficial Activities: Reciting prayers, reading literature that provide inspiration, and lending a helping hand to those who are less fortunate than we are all assist to fill our hearts with compassion, patience, clarity, and love. These are the most straightforward and efficient methods for releasing any restrictions on the natural flow of prana via the heart chakra.

Exercises that focus on breathing may assist us in taming unruly emotions and coming to terms with them. If you do them on a consistent basis, you will see a greater improvement.

The word "YAM" is the mantra that corresponds to this chakra. By repeating this phrase, we are able to rid ourselves of our possessive impulses and understand what it is to "let go." We are able to access the wellspring of love that is inside our hearts by reciting the mantra SO HAM. We acquire the ability to forgive and to forget.

Green is the hue that is often connected with the heart chakra. Crystals such as emeralds, jade, peridots, and rubies are some examples of stones that may assist in the cleansing and healing of this chakra.

Meditation is the most effective method for clearing up this chakra. We progressively learn, during the course of the meditation sessions, to concentrate all of your attention on the wonderful experiences that we have had in the past. Because of this, we are better able to tap into the flow of energy.

When we focus the positive energy that we feel from these recollections on a particular loved one, we are able to strengthen the connection that we have with that person. As we investigate our history, we run the risk of reliving all of the heartache and disappointment we've been through in the past. The strength to face, triumph over, and ultimately 'let go of' these demons will be bestowed to us as we recite the mantra and say our prayers during the whole process.

The sequence of flowing asanas known as khatupranam is designed to act primarily on the anahat chakra. It also contributes to the balancing and harmonizing of the body, mind, and soul.

Opening and Closing Your Chakras is Covered in Chapter 4

Before you make an effort to open your Chakras, it is important to have a fundamental understanding of the Chakras and the colors that are associated with them. Acquiring knowledge of the seven colors, in order from the root to the crown, will enable you to open or close your energy centers without drawing your attention away from the process by reading a list of instructions.

It is essential to make use of visualization while opening and shutting your Chakra points at all times. Relax for a while and try to see different hues in your mind. The numbers one through seven are the ones that stand out most clearly in my mind when I try to picture them. Make the color of each number correspond to the Chakra it represents. When you have the number clearly seen in your mind, try first intensifying the color, and then bringing it back down to its original level.

Try to relax; it will become easier, and before long, you will discover that you can do it without putting too much concentration into it. Although it is acceptable to feel a bit annoyed when doing this, since visualization is not something that comes easily to everyone, it is important to remember that this is normal.

Take a comfortable seat, try to relax, and concentrate on how your breath sounds. Maintain your focus on taking long, slow, and deep breaths in through the nose, followed by breaths out through the mouth. Listening to the sound of your breathing is a great way to clear your thoughts.

You now need to center yourself and get a grip.

An anchoring

Imagine that you have roots growing from your feet all the way down into the earth now that you have succeeded in calming your thoughts. Sense the energy of the ground rising up via your roots and entering your body through your right foot. This energy is coming from the soil.

Permit the energy to flow upwards via your right leg, up through your right side, and all the way up to the top of your head. Then, allow the energy to move downwards down your left hand side and out through your left foot before returning to the ground. Imagine this energy as a current that moves from one part of your body to another in a never-ending loop.

Maintain this visualization of this energy, and maintain the flow of the cycle going at all times. You are now confined.

Activation of the Chakras

Now, in order to open the chakras, you need to imagine this current of white energy moving in a slightly different direction. Put your attention on your root Chakra and imagine it as a dull red shape in the form of the number one.

(When you have gained more experience with this, you will have the ability to switch it from a number to an image of your choosing.)

Observe how the number goes from having a dull red color to having a vivid red color as the energy fills it. (Your previous experience with visualization will be of use to you in this regard, but it may take you a few tries before you are able to concentrate sufficiently to perfect the talent.) Your Chakra point is becoming more accessible as the color of the number increases. After all of the light has been allowed in, it will fully open.

Keep moving upwards until you reach your sacral chakra and continue the flow of energy. Employ the same method of visualization, but this time with the number 2 in a dull orange color. Increase the brightness of the number, and go higher.

Continue to direct the flow of energy through the subsequent Chakras, checking to make sure that the numbers align with the appropriate colors at each one. After you have successfully opened your Crown Chakra, let part of the energy to flow up through the top of your head, then down around you to fill your aura. Do this until the energy no longer flows through you.

Imagine that the outside borders of the aura are gradually becoming more tangible as you continue to do this. Imagine that this is creating a barrier that only pure good energy can pass through, and that this barrier is preventing any negative effects from entering your body. (By doing this, you will be better able to protect yourself from the powerful impacts that come from other people's auras.)

The remaining fifty percent of your energy stream should be directed such that it flows back into the continuous stream and then back out of your right foot. Maintain the cycle, but this time make a little adjustment to its path so that it runs up and across your Chakra points as it makes its way through the cycle.

Bringing the Chakra Points to a Close

Before you bring yourself out of a meditative state, it is important to make sure that your chakras are closed. If you do not seal your chakras at the end of each day, you will leave yourself open to having the energy you have taken from you by people around you who do not have control over their own energy fields.

You should leave them slightly open to enable the continuing of energy to flow unrestrained, but you should make sure to shut the tap sufficiently that it leaves just a steady trickle running until you become skilled at regulating your energy. Leaving them slightly open will allow the continuation of energy to flow unrestricted.

The act of closing your Chakras is analogous to doing the opposite of expanding them. You should begin at the Crown and work your way down to the Root. When shutting, the hue should be toned down rather than brightened.

When shutting, do not entirely shut down the Chakras; rather, you should ensure that a little amount of energy is still steadily moving through each of them. While you are reducing the brightness of the color, go to the next Chakra before you have entirely reduced the brightness of the previous Chakra, leaving it with a dull glow.

Once you feel that you have properly closed down, rest for a few minutes as you gently return your breathing rate to normal.

www.ingramcontent.com/pod-product-compliance
Lightning Source LLC
Chambersburg PA
CBHW050413120526
44590CB00015B/1948